from nothing

POEMS

from nothing

ANYA KRUGOVOY SILVER

Louisiana State University Press   Baton Rouge

Published by Louisiana State University Press
Copyright © 2016 by Anya Krugovoy Silver
All rights reserved
Manufactured in the United States of America
LSU Press Paperback Original
First printing

Designer: Barbara Neely Bourgoyne
Typeface: Livory
Printer and binder: LSI

Library of Congress Cataloging-in-Publication Data
Names: Silver, Anya Krugovoy, 1968– author.
Title: From nothing : poems / Anya Krugovoy Silver.
Description: Baton Rouge : Louisiana State University Press, [2016]
Identifiers: LCCN 2016005175| ISBN 978-0-8071-6346-7 (pbk. : alk
    paper) | ISBN 978-0-8071-6347-4 (pdf) | ISBN 978-0-8071-6348-1
    (epub) | ISBN 978-0-8071-6349-8 (mobi)
Classification: LCC PS3619.I5465 A6 2016 | DDC 811/.6—dc23
LC record available at http://lccn.loc.gov/2016005175

To my mother, Christel,
my sister, Claudia,
and

in memory of my father, Yuri

I hold my head and sing / in this late hour, at daybreak.

—MARINA TSVETAEVA

CONTENTS

III

from nothing

FROM NOTHING

I am re-begot / Of absence, darkness, death: things which are not.
—JOHN DONNE, "A Nocturnal upon St. Lucy's Day"

Again and again, from nothingness I'm born.
Each death I witness makes me more my own.
        I imagine each excess line of mine erased,
        each muscle shredded, each bone sheared.
                One day, my spine's long spar will snap,
ribs tumbling loose; my face will droop and drop.
Then I'll be re-begot—the air will shimmer
and my molecules will vault, emerging free.
From darkening days, the light will surge and flee.

I

SUMMERS IN VERMONT

There were evenings my sister and I
rolled, clover-smudged, down hills,
the sky a red horse pursued by a black.
Magic honey slackened my mother's
shoulder so she could swim again.
During the day, we read first editions
behind curtains, like prim Victorians.

The days were holy,
like the stinging, sacrificial bees,
or the deep lakes we dreamed of,
gleaming in mountains too tall to climb,
and the low voices of Russian refugees
recounting the losses of the exiled.

I remember my parents murmuring
histories I knew I shouldn't hear,
nights when my sister and I lay in our rooms,
she sleeping and me thinking up stories
in which I possessed powers far beyond my own,
able to make the sun blister and the clouds bloom.

PRAYING AS A CHILD

My prayers wrote themselves so easily
on God's body, washing off effortlessly
as colored chalk from my hands.
I thanked God for food and drink
(*für essen und trinken*), and blessed
my family and certain people—Misha
and Natasha—I don't remember.
Fear of wolves, ovens, and spiders
yielded beneath my mother's hand.
No anger rattled the lock on the gate.
There was no knife thrust between God's teeth.
Which is to say, neither was there faith.

COINCIDENCE

The same morning I press my shorn chest
against an X-ray machine and hold my breath,
my sister births from her body a baby girl.
Praise God, whose hands pass over each other
like river currents as they give and take,
pulling one film from the whirring machine
while pushing in a new, unprinted slide.
Praise God for this fearful doubling,
over which I will sometimes weep and curse.
Little breathing at the nursing whole breast
of my sister, little gold seed of death
awakening as the first sun touches its tendrils.

For Claudia Krugovoy

TANTE ANNEL'S SCRAPBOOK

For sixty years, she kept her scrapbook,
this record that bites and scalds my hands.
She took it with her, house to house.
All those delighted revelers, *heil*-ing.
And the prize clipping—a visit from Göring
to Ludwigshafen—the sky aswarm with flags.
Each new page a body dragged from hiding.
"Why?" I ask my uncle, who won't reply.
None of them will, still silent after so long.
"Why do you want to know this *Scheisse*?"
is all my mother says, putting away knives.
In fifth grade, I lay in her lap once, sobbing,
ashamed of my first, guttural tongue,
my speech a dark and seeded loaf.
She smoothed away the past like she smoothed
my hair, plaiting it so it hung down my back.
Now, too, the photograph of uniformed
Uncle Fritz, sent on Easter to the *Heimat*,
and the shots of children posed on rubble,
draw no remark, all the hatreds of history,
artifacts merely, of a gone world, speechless.
And the impatience at my questions,
as if desire for knowledge were accusation:
as if I were blaming the great-aunt I loved,
who saved, also, the telegram inviting her
to join the circus (a dream she kept secret),
who willed me the garnets at my throat,
who left handfuls of cash, brand new Euros,
thrust in the pockets of never-worn coats.

For Annel Hofmann

NETTLE SHIRTS

Hans Christian Andersen, "The Wild Swans"

The pain of the curse is the nettles,
poisonous and filched from graveyards.
We stitch the shirts ourselves—
blisters kindle our hands and feet
and we shed our nails like hulls.
The stories we're told—that toads
turn into poppies if we're good enough,
that flesh-eating witches are cast out
by prayer—are all make-believe.
We live staked to a wood pile.
If those white swans don't save us on time,
we'll be heaps of ash. No reprieve.
So we sew, we sew in secret, we keep silent.

VERMONT, 1981

That summer, one of her friends scissored off my mother's bun.
"It's too hot for long hair," my mother said. "It's too heavy."
She shook her head like the women in shampoo commercials,
like the before-and-after faces I drew on scrap paper,
my elbows gumming to linoleum in the heat.

And the mothers brushed her hair for her and cooed,
tent dresses as loose and fluid over their bellies
as my own body underwater, when I let my muscles go
and floated, open-eyed, in the misty, muddy green,
water suspending me, weightless, in its sling.

REDBUD

The ovoid buds push free
from the tree's bark, the sun lapping
each pink knob open. Spring's pleasure
blushes the park, but some twigs
remain bare, only dry sheathing.
The sun can breathe and breathe on them,
but no flowers will bloom from that parchment
ever again and that's just how the world
works sometimes. Sometimes I see
the lushness and want to strip it clean.

HOW TO UNWANT WHAT THE BODY HAS WANTED

Confuse the body with sugar until the sugar tastes like love.
Let time descend through your nerves till you're numb,
like a bound foot. Pour dirt in the cup of your bra.
Either wander long streets or lock your door.
Eventually, the plugged drain will release its rotting leaves.
Walk into sharp corners, enjoying the displacement of pain.
Maintain *dignity*. Tears are for lost cats and children who've
    stepped on snails.
Oh, what the hell. Go ahead and wail.
Will yourself into stillness. Take root. Let the web of branches
    hold you.
Let silence, like talcum, expand your lungs.
Recite Akhmatova, *Memory of sun seeps from the heart.*
Talk to women whose husbands have deceived them.
Photograph clouds to cover your walls and ceiling.
Lick honey from the boards of the church in which bees have
    built their hive.
Sleep as deeply alive as an acorn in your bed's black earth.
The wolf in your gut is lust-sated. Prepare the cauldron of
    boiling water.
Dance until your body forgets what it wanted.

LUZERNE

Yes, I remember the painted bridge, and the rain,
and my white fur jacket that wasn't real fur.
Yes, I remember the castle ramparts, café umbrellas
open between showers, the apple cake, and Picassos.
Magical city, its mirrors shrank and multiplied us.
Even the graffiti in the alleys seemed witty.

But I think my smiles were false. I think I was tired.
I wanted to stop walking and pretending to be happy.
All that beauty, and yet I limped as though I'd cut
off my own heel to fit another life's slipper.
I kept hearing time consigning me to darkness,
like the bride who hides in a chest and is never found.

But there was my son, my hand in his damp blond hair.
There was poetry, offering itself like a pair of violet shoes.

THE CHRISTMAS HAT

The hat my father bestowed on me was purple felt.
It fit close to my head with a violet bow.
When I put it on that evening, he was pleased—
a girl in a hat is a lovely sight.

My father's hands spoke Russian when he taught.
They rose in delight and sailed like swans' wings.
I can't imagine them nesting the hat in tissue;
the saleswoman must have rested it in its box.

For a moment, my father stopped thinking
about witches and a demonic black cat in Moscow—
stopped, Christmas Eve, searching for monsters.
A daughter in a hat, her smile a passing reprieve.

RAVEN

Tenderly as one cradles a bowl of water,
he embraced me, and we rose upwards.
Black as *night, first mother of songs,*
he opened my mouth and images thronged
around me: some pressed themselves,
like kisses or worn lace, against my arms,
while others I only glimpsed in wing-beat.
Strong as any lover who had caressed me,
he let me sink back into his feathered body
and all the words of his messenger's heart
resolved into chants and burning candles.
Taut, like wires that support high crosses
on Moscow's golden domes, he held me.
When I began weeping, he caught my neck
and shoes in the spacious expansion
of his enormous wings, then set me gently
down in my home, among the sleepers,
and dawn drove a pen into my hand.

II

ANGUISH

Eyes sewn shut,
she was red and fetal,
her skin fine as tissue,
glued together where birth
(as it was) revealed the sinews.
She had already grown a tilted nose,
a lipless mouth, fine sprigs of hair.
I couldn't see the rest of her body,
because the organs had grown outside
her torso and couldn't be repaired.
Some *freak abnormality*, we were told,
so she'd been swaddled in blankets
to keep what was wrong discreet.
I couldn't even touch her hands
or feet, though I brought home
footprints, the length of quarters.

But that wasn't truly anguish.
Those were early contractions.
Anguish began when I passed
a sculpture of mother and child,
just a stone sphere carved within
a cloaking curve of granite.
At that moment, I stumbled,
grief-glutted, blood rushing
thickly out of me, my haunted
womb dropping in my pelvis.

The world for me was nothing,
nothing, the stare of a mole,
the blackout curtains we'd hung
in the nursery, a nail hole.
That stagger, that inability to hold.

3/21/03

PESHAWAR, 2014

Child's blood-soaked sneaker,
raised on a palm for the camera,
what controversy you incite!
Experts write notes about you:
"No, this photograph isn't from *here*,
It's from that *other* massacre,
or from a drone strike last year."
During all the talk, your tongue
has clotted and dried, rusty,
and can't muster a defense.
Lost forever, the nameless girl
who slipped you on in the morning
before running to school, not knowing
how closely the wings of the Angel
were dipping, or how methodically
men dropped bullets in their rifles.

TENEBRAE

Holy Wednesday

Lord, I know that the bitterness is for her own good.
Through the numbness that has made her quadriplegic,
she has drawn nearer to you, has been purged
as with bloodroot of whatever sins still grieved you.
Her pneumonia has sent her to hospice.
Her descent was rapid, she sleeps her morphine dreams.
Thank you, God, for your wisdom that widows,
for the orphans who continue to praise you.
But Lord, despite your love, close your eyes to me.
Pluck her soul from her paralyzed, tumor-choked body.
But spare me your will and secret knowledge.
Let me continue to live, ignorant and erring.

BY OTHER NAMES

grief and triumph were one and perennial,
petals on the same rose,
or the same rose by other names.
            —KELLY CHERRY

When Rachel was dying, and too weak
any longer to sit up when visitors,
crying, came to say their last goodbyes,
she listened to a friend's prayers,
whispered over the hospital bed.
Suddenly, grabbing the woman's arm,
Rachel lifted her head and prayed—
not for herself, but for her friend,
who was so shocked by this last proof
of goodness that she began to weep.

Then Rachel's face settled again,
its petals sweeping back into place,
and she fell, once more, asleep,
while Christ walked toward her,
holding His shears of pity and peace.

BENEDICTION

And so, in the final days,
the substrate falling in her face,
she reached into dream pockets,
fists of oxygen in her lungs.
I am not afraid, she said.
I was trying to tie magic knots
in the threads we'd wrapped
around our fingers, as children will do,
crissrossing yarn into webs.
The knots weren't holding.
I was trying to identify a bird
that had come to rest in the tree
outside my window—a migrator,
blue-headed vireo or yellow-
rumped warbler—what names!
Something amiss in the structure.
All my knots couldn't stop it.
My thirst for life gets deeper
and deeper the less of it remains.
It was a yellow-rumped warbler.
Color is not a great field marker.
Variations in light and shadow
can play tricks on one's sight.
Water brimmed under the bridge
where I used to stand and watch,
after rains, the fallen sticks gather,
moveable dams, temporary.
What was in her pockets?
She kept turning them over.
I was knotting and unknotting.
The dirt is magic, is sacred,
she said. I am not afraid.
Color is not a great field marker.
Water pushed away the twigs.

JUST RED

I stand in Walgreens while my mother sleeps.
The store is fluorescent and almost empty.
My father is ailing in a nursing home,
my friend is dying in the hospital.
What I want tonight is lipstick.
As pure a red as I can find—no coral
undertones, no rust or fawn. Just red.
Ignoring the salespeople, I untwist tubes
and scrawl each color on my wrist,
till the blue veins beneath my skin
disappear behind smeared bars. I select one.
Back in my mother's apartment, silence.
I limn my lips back out of my wan face.
There they are again: smacky and wanting.

THAT WHITE SUSTENANCE

After Emily Dickinson's "Fascicle 640"

Because of your final, fatal crack,
I've put you, golden handle, in the back
of the china cabinet, to which I, only,
hold the key—so no one knows you're there
except for me, and even I forget from day
to day. But when I recall my lips sipping
from your rim, my peace scatters away.
I have to stop and tightly close my eyes
to keep the rising tears inside my lids,
or scurry to the bathroom for a while
so I can weep that you're no longer here.
Never to be replaced with finer ware.
My breath is frost, the porcelain is white.
It rattles in my hands: the loss, the blight.

For Kristin Sanner

POISE

The little ballerina in my cardboard jewelry box
spun en pointe to music on one pale plastic leg.
I wish that I possessed such poise, whirling,
when wounded, to life's wound-up gears,
the clockmaker God of my forty five years.

But I would say, rather, that I am posed.

Just as I know, instinctively, when a camera
focuses on me, so that no shot is truly candid.

I perform cancer.

During infusions, some patients lose their poise
and slump, steroidal, slack or napping.

I will not let myself sleep in public.
The poisons drain into my blood, precious as rubies.
My veins, like a dancer's ankles, crackle.

BRAIN SURGERY

The knife that pierces your skull is ringing.
Nobody can hear it, not even you.
Its voice contains your sons' voices,
your husband's, and your mother's.
It sings in English and in Mandarin.
The voice is the wind over the Pacific,
the creaking of the bridge under which melons grow.
It blows through the spokes of a bicycle.
The voice contains the voices of thousands
of women, your ancestors, the people
who lived on your island before you were born.
The song is a mattress on the floor, a parakeet,
a hymnal, boiled dumplings, physics.
Every particle of the universe hums through
your brain, insisting *live, live, live.*

For Ishiuan Hargrove

MAID MALEEN

Grimms, "Jungfrau Maleen"

After seven years of damp walls, entombed, no more food,
she and her servant knife their way through the stone tower.
Their first glance outside, a shock. All has changed.
The country's burned and smashed, the banners rent.
No one alive in the castle or village, the farms just soot.
No alarms warned them: abandoned by her own father,
the king, who walled his daughter up and forgot.

Eventually, the tale will be made right again.
A prince will fall in love with Maid Maleen, she will prosper
in her gold necklace and never want for food or home.

Rip out the last pages. There will be no wedding today.
The sulfurous fields don't lead to paths or healing rivers.
Never safety again. Once the smoke's in one's lungs,
it remains forever. The charred trees. The murdered bodies.

IN THE SANATORIUM

It was after the war.
My father lay in an Austrian sanatorium,
his lungs full of tuberculosis.
Next to him, a young Soviet veteran
needed to confess to another Russian.
He had done something terrible, he said.
In Kharkov, before the Germans came.
Under orders, he had taken enemies of the state,
shoved them between two stopped trains,
and burned them to death. Then swept away remains.
Could he ever be forgiven for such a sin?

How could he know, that tormented man,
that my father's father was one of the dead?
What chance that these two men would lie,
shushed to sleep by nurses, side by side?

My father, unable to respond, turned his head.
Riven, six more decades, between two ghosts:
one wasted from coughing, pale; one burning.
Both beyond any word he might have spoken.

SNOW WHITE

How lucky to be pretty enough for a glass coffin,
to die with a full face and cheeks like cherry blossoms.
The poisoned apple must taste sweet in her narrow throat.
The dead I've viewed have never looked so lovely,
maybe because all their blood's been drained,
or their hair has lain too stiff and dark against their skin.
Usually, their bodies are very thin—or otherwise, bloated.
I've kissed their cold faces and they don't sit up.
If a pallbearer stumbles, they don't spit out their deaths.
I've never seen a glass coffin; though, as a child, the etchings
of caskets were often my favorites, such tender mourning.
I hoped beauty and sweetness would bring birds to my wake.
But then dying young happened, the spell came true.
Don't clamp satin over my face: simple burning will do.

WAKE

I missed his death, missed holding him
one last time, my arms enfolding him easily,
after he'd lost the bulk of my childhood.
I missed him again, when I beheld the grey body
in the casket that I had wanted to recognize
and embrace, but whose face was stiff and hard
beneath my lips, whose hands were smooth and cold,
not the soft veined hands I'd expected to hold.
I knew when I lay my head on his chest,
briefly alone in the candle-lit sanctuary,
that what I held was no longer my father.
But still, I wept when the remorseless priest
gently pulled the blue shroud over his head,
tucking him in and sealing the steel lid.

In memoriam, George Krugovoy (1924–2012)

SELF-PORTRAIT ON HER SIXTH
WEDDING ANNIVERSARY

> I know I shall not live very long . . . If I've painted three
> good pictures, then I shall leave gladly with flowers in my
> hand and in my hair.
> —PAULA MODERSOHN-BECKER

Though she painted herself life-sized, nude,
her hands nestling her belly as if pregnant,
it wasn't true—she wasn't bearing an infant,
not even certain she wanted to parent,
just *rushing forward*, giving birth to herself.
Amber beads rest between her small breasts
like a blessing for her safe arrival.

Alone in Paris, away from the German moors,
apart from her husband, ensuring her solitude,
she spent the anniversary with brush and palette,
her huge eyes holding a question, a challenge.
Which to get lost in—a painting or a child?
(How one feels the brush, like a bluebird's
feather, slip from the fingers at a waking cry.)

In only one year, she bore a girl.
Reaching for flowers, she stood up from bed,
complained of pain, and died. Her last words,
What a pity, her baby at her side.
She who'd chosen both forms of quickening:
the drying paint, the kicking child.

LEAVINGS

My son runs, slippery, from the bathroom,
dropping the towel from his still-wet body.
Underwear and shorts, he leaves on the bed
or on the floor, as though they leapt off him.
I follow behind, stepping over what he's shed.

Outside, yellow leaves are beginning to yield,
leaving lawns patchworked as a girl's skirt.
On a walk, I plucked a single blonde hair
from my black shirt, and it flew away
like a wild thing, shimmying in the wind.

At home, I shove the peels and cores
of apples down the disposal, a red whirl,
then order my son to pick up his leavings—
towels, pajamas, and inside-out tees.
He loves bare trees with wind shaking them.

My friend, who can hardly breathe now,
whose sight is failing her, says she'll leave
before Christmas—the final leaving,
for which all others are correspondences,
which folds the others in its giant wings.

For Lori Gill Grennan

FOUR PRAYERS FOR FORGIVENESS

The wound is the place where the Light enters you.
—RUMI

Ya Ghaffar: O Forgiver

For centuries, nomads rubbed propolis on wine skins,
smoothing closed the thin cracks in leather
to preserve clean water beneath the desert sun.

The sacs of my lungs are sprinkled with nodes of cancer.
Ya Ghaffar, Forgiver, refine—like the tiny resinous
feet of bees—my tissues, so your name can plume

through my breath honey-sweet, and my lungs bloom
and collapse like white sheets hanging on lines
in the breeze, beneath the trees' orisons.

Ya Ghafur: O Much Forgiving

No wound greater than this—one's own body mutating.
Spiraling chaos, cell piling on cell like too much yeast,
then migrating through the blood, from tissue to tissue,
infecting healthy cells like deformed spores in a field.
From where does this hatred issue?
How hard not to hate the murderer—one's self, that is.
Ya Ghafur, loose light in the deepest lesions, the clogged lymph
and rotting bone—help me forgive this self-betrayal.
Let love release whatever ails me, and the deepest
pits scar over with a web of luminous silk.

Ya Tawwab: O Relenting

I turn away from cancer. For a moment, it ceases to exist.
My body is clear and slim as a test tube. While I twist,

God turns His face toward me. Wherever I spin, God spins
too, wherever I look, God's presence meets my eyes.
My arm sweeps the air—God makes room for its movement.
If I keep myself attuned to the God-air around me,
the cancer will cease to matter, it will shrink to a slight smudge
at the side of my vision that I can nudge out of view.
So I whirl until I'm dizzy. God dances with me,
matching my bare feet, my wrists, my slender waist.

Ya Affuw: O Effacer

Ya Affuw. The "u" extends on my breath
as though I were blowing colored chalk.
When I exhale out of my heart, I erase the marks
of illness that scar my body. Sickness remains,
but I don't see it—the scattered lumps in my lungs
become church domes roofed in gilded mosaics,
my bones' fissures fill in with grass-green yarn.
All the window panes are gone. It is summer again,
always, and a faint breeze continually wafts the *I*
out of the way—I am absorbed like a drop of water
into a bottle of perfume without a bottom.
I open my eyes and all is golden.

COMES A DAY

After dark vapours have oppressed our plains
For a long dreary season, comes a day
Born of the gentle South and clears away
From the sick heavens all unseemly stains.
                    —JOHN KEATS

And a long, dreary season it's been, all spring,
the names of the dying repeating themselves,
multiplying, *Vicky, Kelly, Kore*, incantatory.
Their names rain hard, brief storms, the kind
that slow down till they're just a dripping
gutter and cloud-cover till the next downpour.
I stay inside, watching through the window.
Yes, the heavens have been sick, and stained
with vomit, blood, and diarrhea. Dirty sheets
stretched over hospital beds, sheets of rain
at the window, low grey clouds, grey ash
urned in the hands of the grieving husband
who texts his wife before remembering
that she's dead. *It's just a habit*, he weeps.
Come, gentle South, and sweep them away,
not the women or their ashes, which must stay
on Earth, but the deaths, the downturns.
Let's talk only of the sky, the blue, the robins.
How the trees hold them, hold them, let them go.

In memory of Vicky, Kelly, and Kore

DANNON

When you were first diagnosed with cancer,
a commercial for yogurt made you furious—
that others could think about pureed fruit
when you might be dying! The woman
shimmying across the screen, smiling,
orgasmic even, as though she had found
the answer to life's puzzles in probiotics.

Now, all these years later, you've eased back
into the banal. Let women sing the praises
of yogurt, tampons, and long-lash mascara!
Let them find comfort in whole-grain bread!
You'd poked your head out of the universe
like an astronomer in medieval engravings,
had begun to see the world's flimsy levees
from the other side—but life sucked you back
with its sticky paws and flung you down
in the muck, as if nothing had changed.

But no need to be dour—your hour hasn't come yet.
Go ahead and eat some lemon yogurt.
Stick your tongue in the little white cup
and lick the whole thing spotless.

AFTER A FAVORABLE PET SCAN

> Yes, you Arcadians will sing
> This tale to your mountains;
> Arcadians only know how to sing.
> —VIRGIL, *Eclogues*

Every moment a Golden Age
to which I've returned from the snare,
my hair beneath the shower
drenched with steaming water,
and summer singing its tale
of cicadas and lawn sprinklers.

Every fruit fills my mouth
with joy—these plums, cherries,
juice after the drought—
the stains they leave on my skirts,
the strands of peach in my teeth.

I want to sing a new song!
For every breath to be thankfulness,
for everything I touch to shiver with life
like the electrical wires that quiver
beneath a squirrel's nimble feet.

Oh world, I will give you all my love.
I will race like a child through the fields,
I will chase off the unkindness of ravens.
My words will grow thick as marshes,
sheltering nests in salty streams.

For You, God, have done this thing for me,
restored me again, like the mounds
of lavender crowned with purple stalks

that sway on the wall all summer long.
Bees, hummingbirds, butterflies,
stay and drink from my sugared throat!
Let me live on the earth forever!

III

E-MAIL FROM MY FIRST BOYFRIEND

To learn that he remembers that trip—
Beethoven's piano in Bonn, the Kölner Dom,
with its tacky hologram postcards of Christ
on the cross, even the plates of Wurstsalat—
means his memory hasn't slammed shut
its matchbox and left me cold and unstruck.
Clearly the mind is too crammed, he writes.
After our breakup came law school, a wife,
three children—but even so, retreading
the Rhine last summer, he glimpsed on a hill
the restaurant where we'd eaten ourselves full.
He must have seen me again, eighteen,
blonde as the Lorelei and reeling with love.

In Hamburg, we gazed at Friedrich's great
paintings, all those ruins, tides, and moonlight,
as though the artist had painted with us in mind:
the alpine blasts of our emotions, our grand
longing for the future, and the deep thrill I felt,
each night, lying in some cheap hotel room.
But my boyfriend wouldn't make love to me.
Not till marriage, he said, and I so needy.

But I'm content now to exist as reverie.
I'm squinting in the sunshine, wearing a straw hat
and a yellow and white skirt, looking as I looked
that summer years ago—eager, mistaken, open,
sated with roasted potatoes and cherry cake.

PARTINGS

My uncle said goodbye to each piece of furniture
he left at the curb after my grandfather's death,
poor wares he couldn't resell: the rotting bamboo
doors of the china cabinet, postwar bookshelves.
To each and every item, he wished farewell.
Months later, he received, from Poland, a snapshot
of the old sofa, re-upholstered, in a handsome room,
with a note of thanks from the new owner.
Just so, I leaned over the casket and kissed my father,
empty now as a glass with a slight, invisible crack,
out of which his life had seeped for years.
But when I dreamed of him, he stood tall again,
so tall that, like a child, I could no longer see his face.
But he embraced me. He said, *My new home is good.*

WOMAN WITH A HOLE IN HER STOCKING

Such a universal female gesture,
a woman grabbing the seam of her stocking,
tugging it forward over the exposed toe,
tucking it under her foot so the tear won't show.
There's something graceful and humble
about the way she will balance, crane-like,
on one foot, cradling the other in her hand,
her back bent, her face tilted downward,
trying to hide the damage of the splintered
floorboard, or untrimmed toenail.
Sometimes, while she's leaning over,
a strand will float loose from its ponytail.
Then she'll stand, recombing her hair
with her hands, repair after tiny repair.

GARDEN FLOWERS, WATERCOLOR

Emil Nolde

I am the red foxglove with its indigo center,
the blurred bunches of Canterbury bells.
I am the orange poppies called *Mohn,*
which also means *moon,* which turns me.
In your arms, I deepen to crimson.
My center is a black well I cannot plumb.
I powder with pollen your lips and brow,
turn my face toward you like a prow.
But where are you, my love? In the heavy
storm clouds over the northern sea.
Come shred my petals, tear them free.

RED NEVER LASTS

There's no doubt it's the most glamorous,
the one you reach for first—its luscious gloss.
Russian Roulette, First Dance, Apéritif, Cherry Pop.
For three days, your nails are a Ferris wheel,
a field of roses, a flashing neon *Open* sign.
Whatever you're wearing feels like a tight dress
and your hair tousles like Marilyn's on the beach.
But soon, after dishwashing, typing, mopping,
the chips begin, first at the very tips and edges
where you hardly notice, then whole shards.
Eventually, the fuss is too much to maintain.
Time to settle in to the neutral tones.
Baby's Breath, Curtain Call, Bone.

TO LANA DEL REY AT FIFTY

Will you still love me when I shine from words and not from beauty?
—LANA DEL REY, "Old Money"

Turn your back on the photographers waiting outside the hospital.
Or do you still crave the flashes? The hand on your throat,
white bikinis, lovers who tore you in half like an orange.
You're beautiful, my love. Your lips drive me insane.
How gradually women's bodies disappear,
men's glances ebbing each year, shifting past our shoulders.
We draw the loose skin of our necks back with our thumbs.
I can't wait till Sunday so I can pray to Lana. I'll come to you, Lana.
We line our lips in cranberry, brush our eyelids heavy gold.
We swear we can hold another glass of wine, then stumble.

Lana, you can still pretend you're free. Light up a cigarette.
Paint your nails black. Acrylic lasts.

PROMENADE

Marc Chagall, 1917

While he holds her hand, his bride hovers
above him, fluttering like festal streamers.
Over the crooked green houses, she drifts,
sailing past the church's dreaming domes.
Frightening to imagine how easily he could let her go,
how quickly she would whirl beyond his reach.
Only a single hand yokes her body to earth.
She's so light, all mass blown out of her bones
as though she were an egg, emptied by breath.
But her husband won't forsake her. They've shared
a heap of red tablecloth, plum cake, wine.
A blue tree blossoms, longing, towards them.

ASH WEDNESDAY, UNSHOWERED

My hair's pulled back to disguise the grime,
though maybe it's well that I'm unclean,
since *from dust you came, to dust you will return,*
the priest recites, smearing my forehead.
Once, twice, and I'm marked, a lintel in plague years.
I'm invited to kneel and read the fifty-first Psalm,
recalling how David watched Bathsheba bathe.
Cleanse me with hyssop, and I will be clean;
wash me, and I will be whiter than snow.
Merciful One, save me from slight repentance.
I pierced the center of the white orchid, Lord,
and it was mud, blood's cry, my body's blighted tender.

ST. PAUL'S LETTER TO THE EPHESIANS, LENT

At the word *fornicators,* I roll my eyes.
Not to live in the passions of the flesh—
how grim and arid the light we're promised,
as if all the earth were bleak midwinter.
Meanwhile, Paul, plum trees are bruising
the church parking lot, cherry trees readying
their exuberant and joyful climax of pink,
the palest pink, nipple-pink, pink of my dry
(I lick them) lips, of my amoral animal body.
Not easily have I obeyed the commandments.
For I love that keen, painful twisting of desire,
the tight bud of it straining against its husk.

WISTERIA

She thought it was impossible, ludicrous,
grotesque even—she already forty-five
and disfigured—that it was lost for good.
She hadn't wanted to let it go, had wrenched hard
to keep it, had wept, gone stiff and angry.
But it was shadow, enigma, gnawed up, gone.
And then, suddenly, he was back, the bark
she had traced so wistfully bearing blossom.
Wisteria hung opulent from the wire fence,
papery petals sweating sugar. Yes, she had it again.
Temporary, but no matter. It had returned to her.
She forgot how to speak: she crammed; she raved.

KLIMT, *RECUMBENT LOVERS*

Like roots, they have grown into each other,
a series of curves and intertwinings,
of clutching and resting arms and legs.
Her closed eyes are all we see of her face.
This, love, is what I want for us:
the doubling, clasping, the wet stillness
following rapid movement, like the deeper
sinking into sleep after a dream, the erasure
of goal, end point, time, anticipation.
Just our two bodies immersed in each other,
the way I tell you I like to approach the sea,
with closed eyes, so that I can hear the tides
come, then slip away, and smell the brine
on my skin, and taste the salt with each lick
of my lips as I lie, knees bent, in waves
as each one pulls me farther from the shore.

SATURDAY MORNINGS

Toulouse-Lautrec, In Bed, *1897*

How can I tell the truth about twenty years of loving?
Toulouse-Lautrec portrayed it best with his couple
lying in bed together: two dark, uncombed heads
leaning against pillows, just talking to each other,
sleepily, peeping out beneath the heap of blankets.
Saturday mornings, underneath the comforter,
our feet touch each other, sharing the down's heat,
while we compare last night's dreams, or prepare days.
By evening, we'll have forgotten much of what we say.
But the sun shows palest pink through window blinds,
and if you wanted to, you could reach out and twine
my hair, or I could find the hidden cleft inside your ear.
There would be no fear or self-consciousness at all,
our lives a loom and we, the warp, the weft.

AT THE STATION

When the girl got off the train at the college town,
she leapt up and wrapped her legs around the waist
of the boy she'd come to visit, and they spun
around, embracing and shrieking with joy.
Their love set off a piccolo's vibration.
Those years are gone for us—I see you every day,
we eat meals together from decades-old plates.
But when we lie in bed at night, you take my hand,
and I feel the orb that's formed around us tighten,
while you and I, like knitting needles in a ball
of yarn, lie beside each other, fingers touching.

KORE

She climbs out of the hole in the earth where she was taken.
Roots scrape and scratch her bare legs, snap against her skin.
Her calves are smeared with soil, her fingertips ringed with jet
from clawing her way up the ladderless underground banks.
The shaft is ringed with weeping grasses, weeds that disguise
the pit beneath them; they push against her, their sap
slicking her hands as she heaves herself out,
slinging her leg over the sides and swinging over.
Instantly, her shorn head comes alive, curls
forcing themselves through her bald skull.
She strips off her shroud and stands bare in the field.
Scarred with struggle, she has six months before she returns.
She shakes her beautiful summer hair.

AUTUMN

Shake the wild apple tree.
Remove the bread from the oven before it burns,
then cross yourself as you cut the loaf.
The dead have bloodied the maple's branch.
Ruin is more beautiful than drooping July.
Sleeplessness purples my eyes, crows cast shadows.
The mockingbird continues its monologue,
as though summer weren't already stalking
like a cat around the corner, swishing its tail.

IDEAL SPEECH

My whole life was language.
—FRIEDERIKE MAYRÖCKER

The whole world is a whorled apple, peeled
and ever peeling, apple whose core is God,
our speech just a shadow of ideal speech,
paring deeper but never reaching the center.

(Witch hazel's thready yellow bloom, sweet
yellow lashes in the park, redbuds splitting
through bark as though impatient for twigs,
how I love the many-fingered body of this world.)

Listen to the Holy Ghost. She blows through you,
she blows her poems right through.

THREE ROSES

Where only my scar line remains, a red rose blooms.
Luscious, full, so open that if it dropped a single petal,
it would not be as lovely as it is this very moment.
My eyes watch through the rose's flaming center,
crimson, as if through a hundred desiring eyes,
till the world prisms: quartz pink, blush, vermillion.

Where my right breast remains, a white rose grows.
Satin, milk-soaked lace, a newborn ewe's plush.
Opening like something too pure to be touched,
but eager to be touched, soft as talcum to the finger.
An infant could linger at its billowing petals.
All cries would be stilled at that sugared font.

In my sternum grows the rarest rose of all—
the gold rose, not plucked in any human garden.
It spreads petals in the chambers of my heart,
gold touching every dark cell of my body with love.
Lay your hands on my chest—here, I give it to you.
Feel your palm on my skin heat and spark.

ACKNOWLEDGEMENTS

Thank you to these journals in which the following poems first appeared, sometimes with different titles:

America: "From Nothing"; *Atlanta Review:* "Autumn," "Benediction," and "Red Never Lasts"; *Bread and Glitter:* "Praying as a Child"; *Calamaro:* "Peshawar, 2014"; *The Christian Century:* "Coincidence"; *The Cossack Review:* "St. Paul's Letter to the Ephesians, Lent"; *Crab Orchard Review:* "Vermont, 1981"; *Five Points:* "Luzerne," "How to Unwant What the Body Has Wanted," and "Tante Annel's Scrapbook"; *Ginosko Journal:* "Summers in Vermont," "Wake" (as "My Father's Voice), and "Woman With a Hole in Her Stocking"; *Harvard Review:* "Maid Maleen" and "Snow White"; *Image:* "Ash Wednesday, Unshowered," "By Other Names," "Raven," "Tenebrae," and "Three Roses"; *Iron Horse Review:* "Klimt, *Recumbent Lovers*"; *New Ohio Review:* "Dannon"; *New South:* "Leavings"; *Poet Lore:* "At the Station"; *Rock and Sling:* "After a Favorable PET Scan" and "Four Prayers for Forgiveness"; *Shenandoah:* "That White Sustenance"; *Southern Poetry Review:* "Redbud"; *St. Katherine Review:* "Anguish" and "Ideal Speech."

"Tante Annel's Scrapbook" was also published on Poetry Daily, www.poems .com.

"At the Sanatorium" was published by the Academy of American Poets as a Poem-A-Day.

"E-mail from my First Boyfriend" was published in the anthology *Intimacy: An Anthology* (Jacar Press, 2015).

"Maid Maleen" was also published in *Best American Poetry 2016*, ed. David Lehman and Edward Hirsch.

This book would not have been published without the commitment to poetry of LSU Press. Thank you so much to MaryKatherine Callaway and John Easterly for your generosity and kindness. Thank you also to Neal Novak for such careful editing.

Thank you to the following friends and writers who helped me invaluably and generously with this manuscript, with its individual poems, or by organizing readings for me: Kathryn Stripling Byer, Claire Bateman, Nicole Cooley, Terri Erickson, Alice Friman, Megan Sexton, Tamar Perla, Gary Ballard, and William Woolfitt. Thanks to Jeanie Tomanek for graciously supplying the painting on the book's cover and for the inspiration of her beautiful work.

This book is also in memory of my friends who have died from metastatic breast cancer: Kristin Sanner, Lori Gill Grennan, Paula Ford, Vicky Keys, Kelly Sullivan Kimball, Nathalie Priemer, Susan Freed, Suzanne Lemay, Marie Anello-Algeri, Mary Ann Valaitis Whaley, Paula Draper, LeeAnn Elgin, Hollie Jeffers, Evon Miller, Kore Bormann, Christy Bailey, and all those whom I haven't named or who died after this book went to press. May their memories be eternal.

To my fellow travelers on this difficult journey: Ishiuan Hargrove, Kathleen Strosser, Terry Arnold, Holli Durkin, Jane Carder, Phyllis Johnson, Jenee Boborra, Ginny Mason, and all those whom I haven't mentioned because the list would get too long.

Mercer University has enabled me to write this book despite the complications of my treatment. Thanks especially to my department chair and friend Gary Richardson and to Dean Lake Lambert, both of whom always put my health and well-being before their administrative needs. Thanks also to the many students who helped bring meaning to my life. Yes, I have favorites. You know who you are. You have lifted me up day after day.

Special thanks for friendship to four of my guardian angels: Sarah Gerwig, Sara Hughes, Sara Walcott, and Oonie Lynch. You have been there for me always, and I treasure and love you.

This book is dedicated to my sister, best friend, and soeurilein Claudia, my sweet and gentle Muttichen, and my devoted and inspirational late father with my great, enduring love for teaching me the values of kindness, thankfulness, beauty, reading, and a happy family. Words can't do the depth of my love justice.

Wenn du Märchenaugen hast, ist die Welt voller Wunder.

—VICTOR BLÜTHGEN

And to my husband and soulmate, Andy, and my precious son, Noah, my beloveds and centers of my being. Thank you for accompanying me through this most amazing and extraordinarily blessed life, and for holding me up during times of suffering. I love you as much as it is possible to love. I will always be with you. In the other world, forever.

> He heals the brokenhearted,
> and binds up their wounds.
> He determines the number of the stars,
> he gives to all of them their names.
>
> PSALM 147

NOTES

"I hold my head and sing . . .": Marina Tsvetaeva, from *Marina Tsvetaeva: Selected Poems*, trans. Elaine Feinstein.

"From Nothing": The entire title of the John Donne poem is "A Nocturnal upon St. Lucy's Day, Being the Shortest Day." St. Lucy is traditionally associated with light; her name derives from the Latin *lucis*, or light.

"How to Unwant What the Body Has Wanted" is a line from the Cecilia Woloch poem, "Postcard Beginning with a Quote from Marc C., Avenue de l'Opéra," from her book *Carpathia*.

"The Christmas Hat": The allusion to the demonic cat in the poem was inspired by Mikhail Bulgakov's novel *The Master and Margarita*.

"Raven": The italicized portion of the line is from Marina Tsvetaeva's "Insomnia," trans. Elaine Feinstein.

"Maid Maleen": "There will be no wedding today" is a line from Brontë's *Jane Eyre*.

"Four Prayers for Forgiveness" and "Three Roses" are inspired by Sufi meditations.

"Woman with a Hole in Her Stocking" is based on the painting *Girl with a Hole in Her Stocking* by Michael Thompson (1998).

"To Lana Del Rey at Fifty": Lana Del Rey is a pop singer. The first line of the poem is an allusion to Marilyn Monroe in the hospital after having had a miscarriage. Monroe turned her back to the paparazzi outside her window.

"Autumn": It was a folk tradition in Russia to cross a loaf of bread while cutting it lest evil spirits had entered the bubbles in the dough.

CPSIA information can be obtained
at www.ICGtesting.com
Printed in the USA
LVOW11s1925270318
571328LV00005B/757/P